Spot the Difference

Fruits

Charlotte Guillain

Heinemann Library
Chicago, Illinois

Customer Service 888-454-2279
Visit our website at www.heinemannraintree.com

Designed by Joanna Hinton-Malivoire
Photo research by Erica Martin and Hannah Taylor
Printed and bound in China by South China Printing Co. Ltd.
12 11 10 09 08
10 9 8 7 6 5 4 3 2 1

Library of Congress Cataloging-in-Publication Data

Guillain, Charlotte.
Fruits / Charlotte Guillain. -- 1st ed.
p. cm. -- (Spot the difference)
Includes index.
ISBN-13: 978-1-4329-0947-5 (library binding-hardcover)
ISBN-10: 1-4329-0947-9 (library binding-hardcover)
ISBN-13: 978-1-4329-0954-3 (pbk.)
ISBN-10: 1-4329-0954-1 (pbk.)
1. Fruit--Juvenile literature. I. Title.
QK660.G83 2008
581.4'64--dc22

2007035918

Acknowledgements
The publishers would like to thank the following for permission to reproduce photographs: ©FLPA pp.**17**, **18** (Jurgen & Christine Sohns), **8** (Bjorn Ullhagen), **9** (Gary K Smith), **15**, **23 bottom** (Holt/Primrose Peacock), **6, 14** (Nigel Cattlin), **19**, **23 middle** (Parameswaran Pillai Karunakaran); ©istockphoto.com pp.**4 bottom right** (Stan Rohrer), **4 top left** (CHEN PING-HUNG), **4 top right** (John Pitcher), **4 bottom left** (Vladimir Ivanov), **16 inset** (Yong Hian Lim); ©Nature Picture Library pp.**5** (De Meester / ARCO), **13** (Gary K. Smith), **7** (Mark Payne-Gill), **21** (Tony Evans); ©Photolibrary pp.**11**, **22 left** (Foodpix), **10** (Botanica), **20**, **23 top** (Images.Com), **16** (Michele Lamontagne), **12, 22 right** (Pacific Stock).

Cover photograph of lemons reproduced with permission of ©Photolibrary (Guy Moberly). Back cover photograph of a pineapple reproduced with permission of ©Photolibrary (Pacific Stock).

Contents

What Are Plants?

Plants are living things.
Plants live in many places.

Plants need air to grow.
Plants need water to grow.
Plants need sunlight to grow.

What Are Fruits?

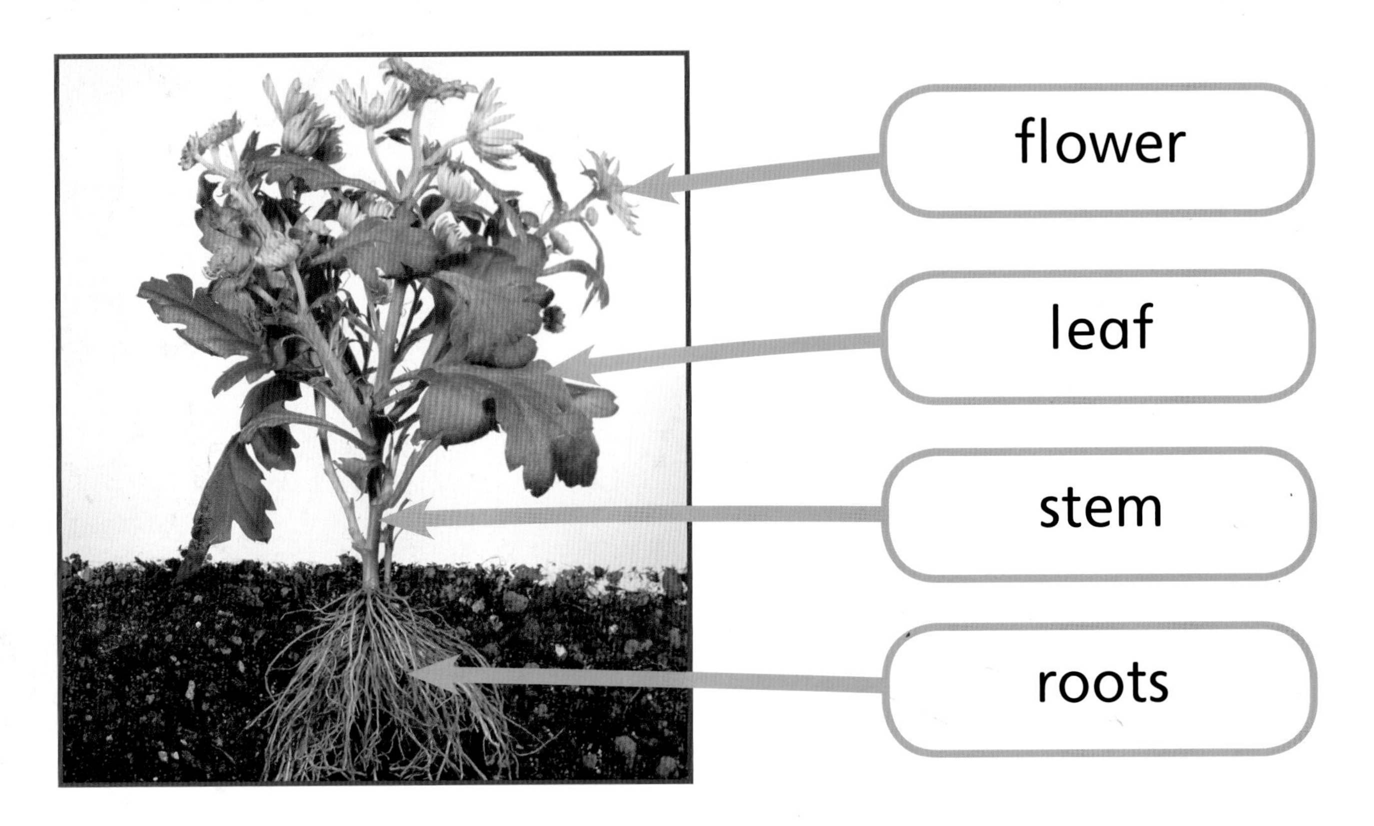

Plants have many parts.

Many plants have fruits.

Different Fruits

This is an apple tree.
Its fruit is red.

This is a plum tree.
Its fruit is purple.

This is a mango tree.
Its fruit is smooth.

This is a lychee tree.
Its fruit is rough.

This is a pineapple plant.
It has one large fruit.

This is a blackberry plant.
It has many small fruits.

Amazing Fruits

This is a rambutan.
It is a hairy fruit.

This is a thornapple.
It is a spiky fruit.

This is a starfruit.
It is a star shape.

This is a sausage fruit.
It is a long shape.

These are jack fruits.
They taste sweet.

These are passion fruits.
They taste sour.

What Do Fruits Do?

Fruits have seeds.

Seeds grow into new plants.

Spot the Difference!

How many differences can you see?

Picture Glossary

fruit the part of a plant which holds seeds

sour has a bitter taste

spiky has sharp points

Index

Note to Parents and Teachers

Before reading
Show the children some different fruits (e.g. apple, orange, banana). Cut them in half and show them the seeds. Explain that the fruit protects the seed while it is growing. When the seed is ripe, the fruit falls from the plant.

After reading
- Cut several fruits into small pieces and place each fruit in a plastic box. Do not show the children the fruit. Select a plastic box and challenge the children to ask questions about the fruit, such as: Is it red? Is it soft? When the children have guessed the fruit correctly they can each have a taste.
- Make card templates of some fruits (e.g. apple, pear, banana, orange, plum). Tell the children to choose a fruit and to draw around the template onto thin card. They should cut out the fruit and color it in the appropriate color. Suspend the fruit from a coat hanger to make a fruit mobile.